Orange in My World

By Brienna Rossiter

level
1
little blue
readers

www.littlebluehousebooks.com

Little Blue House is distributed by North Star Editions:
sales@northstareditions.com | 888-417-0195

Produced for Little Blue House by Red Line Editorial.

Photographs ©: Shutterstock Images, cover, 4, 6–7, 12–13, 15, 16 (top left), 16 (top right), 16 (bottom left), 16 (bottom right); iStockphoto, 8–9, 11

Library of Congress Control Number: 2020900860

ISBN
978-1-64619-159-8 (hardcover)
978-1-64619-193-2 (paperback)
978-1-64619-261-8 (ebook pdf)
978-1-64619-227-4 (hosted ebook)

Printed in the United States of America
Mankato, MN
082020

About the Author

Brienna Rossiter enjoys playing music, reading books, and drinking tea. She lives in Minnesota.

Table of Contents

I See Orange

I drink juice with

my breakfast.

The juice is orange.

I pack my clothes for a trip.

My suitcase is orange.

I go camping in
the woods.

My tent is orange.

I sit in a boat.

My life jacket is orange.

life jacket

I sit by a fire.

I watch the fire.

The fire is orange.

The day is almost over.

The sun sets.

The sky is orange.

Glossary

clothes

life jacket

fire

tent

Index